TALKING SMACK TO THE DEAD

POETRY & PROSE

A shotgun-seat ride to the tragedy of Shanksville, Flight 93 with
James Dean, Euterpe the muse, a redneck driving a Dodge Hemi
pickup, Donna Mae and others.

WALT PETERSON

Copyright © 2022 WALT PETERSON
COVER: CYBERWIT
ISBN: 978-81-8253-904-4

First Edition: 2022
Rs. 200/-

Cyberwit.net
HIG 45 Kaushambi Kunj, Kalindipuram
Allahabad - 211011 (U.P.) India
http://www.cyberwit.net
Tel: +(91) 9415091004
E-mail: info@cyberwit.net

Printed at VCORE CONNECT LLP.

READING PETERSON

I have been eating fish I caught myself for five weeks, so I went to a bar for a burger and opened your book (*Depth-of-Field*) & knew from the first page it was beautifully written.

—Stuart Dybek, *I Sailed With Magellan*, Farrar, Straus and Giroux

"Music, sweet Sister, is winter rain/ hissing from eighteen wheels/ on the interstate."

In Walt Peterson's *Talking Smack to the Dead*, a collection of poetry and prose is a vivid view of those who drive trucks, race cars, who spend their lives on the dangerous roads of western Pennsylvania, in the grimy motels and repair shops on the roadsides. Voices have an authentic working-class tone and diction. We ride through a car wash and learn the sensuous pleasure of Negro spirituals. We even hear a pet chicken's account of interrupting his owner's tryst. There is something to delight every reader in this fine, varied collection.

—Paul Wilson, *Chrome Dreams*: *Automobile Styling Since 1893*

How to Read Walt Peterson

Pick this book up off the passenger seat, and open its pages with the other hand on the steering wheel. This collection is the flash of time before a crash, wonderful, slow, sensory. The impression *Talking Smack to the Dead* leaves on you is the impression your fist left on the dashboard, the bruise on your shoulder from the seatbelt, the deafening silence where the motor once roared. Check your mirrors. Step out. Sit on the guard rail. Turn these pages gently, slowly—there's no rush now.

—David Stuursma, Editor, *Moss Motoring*

Talking Smack to the Dead by Walt Peterson runs low and hot through the land of adrenalin. These are hemi-powered poems, lines of tripped-out rhythms… stainless saddle tanks/fill with diesel fuel and chrome exhaust stacks blue with the heat of the night's passage… Peterson writes the memorial "Shanksville" running high-throttle emotion into restless heart, delivering us to wild tenderness.

—Jan Beatty, *The Body Wars*, University of Pittsburgh Press

IN GRATITUDE

For Jade, ace reader and my wing-girl in heart-stopping drives.

For Pittsburgh Poetry Exchange: Michael, Ziggy, Judith, Arlene, Barry, Frank, Stuart, et al.

For Jan B., for Joan Bauer for keeping the oral tradition alive at Hemingway's.

For the Western Pennsylvania Writing Project, Sam Hazo, Stuart Dybek and Chris Wolf.

For the accomplishments of Mark Donohue, Michele Mouton, Pat Moss, Mark Abele, Mario Andretti, Juan Manuel Fangio, Robert Kubica. Kent Rafferty, Mike Ancas. For Denise McCluggage, automotive journalist and competent driver on an international level.

For Michael Wurster

and

Len Roberts, in memoriam

Brothers in word and in deed.

There was no where to go but everywhere, so just keep rolling under the stars.

—Jack Kerouac, *On the Road*

La macchina va dove vanno gli occhi.

—Garth Stein, *The Art of Racing in the Rain*

Contents

Part of what we pay is for the car.

Part is to be told who we are.

—Miller Williams

TWO-LANE BLACKTOP

What I need to know, countryboy
—are you in or are you out?
And, no, we don't street race
for drugs or pink slips—I don't
want your race car.

Up Route 10 they said
we'd find real race cars here. What
Pam and I see are sad, slow
pieces of shit with orange-peel paint.
Man, even semi's haulin' pigs to Fort Smith
don't have time to stop for coffee here.

Yeah, that's my Camaro, primered
like they did back in the day.
We baptized the big-block with oil
then drove Cinderella over dusty roads for
that working-girl look.
She's got a T5-6 backed by a Ford nine-inch, topped
it with dual Quadrajets.
Bring on what you got: roadster, gasser, pro-street!

Sweet Pamela? I met her in a backwater
Pennsylvania town. When Dad died, I was nineteen.
We hit the road with what he left, a set of Craftsman tools,
a rusty Buick. Pam does the arm-drop.
We flip for lane choice, straight up, no break-out,
one run takes all. If cops come, it's everyman for himself.

You're lookin' at our fine leather
coats? Took them from two dealers in East L.A.
who thought they could drive. See,
the pockets are slits to trigger sawed-off shotguns.
We're all business. Remember,
when the arms drop, the bullshit stops. There
ain't no peace, no sanctuary here; just the rumble
and rev of engines, headlights high showin' two-lane blacktop.

When Pam raises her arms for the drop,
don't get interested. More than one hick
took too long a look, lost off the line gawkin'
when he mighta', coulda', shoulda' been racin'.

Now, before Barney Fife comes to roll up
sidewalks in this town, make up your mind, rube
—are you in or are you out?
Pony-up, strap in, shut up, hang on.

BLACKED-OUT CHROME, 1945

The table in the kitchen
will soon be set with eggs, Easter bread
and ham. My grandparents, me,
my kid sister stand outside.
Grandfather's hand
on my shoulder and my sister
has a purse and that stupid hat.
The dog is there, too. He looks like
Lassie and his name ends in *e*.
Uncle told me dogs hear that sound better.
The '42 Chevy
with blacked-out chrome
is parked in the background.
At the bottom edge the sidewalk and flowers
just sneak in.
The smell of geraniums and the bread not eaten,
the roughness of brown laundry soap
remind me of my grandmother.

But those in the picture do not exist.
I have never been there to eat the bread
nor smell the geraniums.
We are variations of light impressed upon
photographic paper, the shadow on the steps
in Hiroshima. I say: Here
I am/there they were. Here are you;
the shutter closes with a sharp, metallic click.

APPALACHIAN SUITE

Music,
Sweetest Sister, in this poem
is winter rain hissing from eighteen wheels
on the interstate.
The green glow of the instrument cluster
ghosts a face high in the cab.
White lines are tracer bullets
fired into the fierce lyric of this engine.

Off on a Pennsylvania hill,
a house sings through a single golden window:
loneliness is stern and unforgiving
as the anthracite darkness
of one winter night.

The liner blinks its amber lights and is gone,

but when you awaken, Muse,
there will be music still
as stainless saddle tanks
fill with diesel fuel and chrome exhaust stacks
blue with the heat of the night passage and
crackle as they cool. Then Apollo plays
his light on the Kenworth logo in Georgia dawn.

HAZELWOOD

Through the door at Abriola Auto Parts
you see a rock the size of a loaf of bread
jammed in the wall.

Down the aisles of Brakekleen, starting fluid and Prestone
then the counter man says, *The rock! Oh, you saw it?*

Do I get the prize?

He looks sad to disappoint.
Just the story how I cut my nose off.
The second time those sons-of-bitches
broke in, I rigged tripwires down all the aisles. Those
crooks would find more than brake pads and car shampoo!

You were in 'Nam?

He doesn't answer.

Next morning when we came in, my partner went for the lights,
I, I charged down the aisle. So help me, I just forgot.

The partsman's name was John.

John didn't have the black-oxide, intake manifold bolts I was after
…but, I got more stories if you want to hear 'em.

The surgeon did a fantastic job—
only a hair-wide white line around

the bulb he reattached to John's nose
like the one we all have
at the end of our nose.

BRAILLE RALLY

So Sam says, Hell, man, they ain't gonna know. They're blind, remember?

Sam, a blonde Brillo pad halo of hair, crooked teeth and (this once) impeccable logic. Still, I'm reluctant as a rusted lugnut on a flat tire at night on a rural road in the rain to take a kid from the School for the Blind for a spin over hill, dale and stream then pretend we are in a real performance rally.

But Sam's right, my friend was right!

Little Emma's fingers were birds of prey skimming over the Braille Western Pennsylvania landscape:

Zero your trip odometer.

(What's a trip odometer, Mr. Pete?)

Right turn out of the parking lot.

Proceed 3.7 miles. After the "S" curve, look for the "Caution" sign.

My pal Sam drove a car named after a spaceship, X/11, like a space cowboy—*Here hold my beer and watch this*! Everybody's crazy hero with a party garage complete with a barrel of beer, a kerosene heater and girls, and he's remindin' me that my Chevy Citation, pedestrian grey, four-cylinder, GM's answer to mediocrity and the '80s gas crunch will do just splendidly for this Corporal Work of Mercy. I don't remember Sister Rose saying, "Blessed are the blind, 'cause you can scare the shit out of them." was any part of the Sermon on the Mount.

Thirty miles into that rural night, a rusted rear brake line decided to rupture and getting that gutless wonder of a car stopped became more than interesting, but there's still the front braking circuit, so we limped back to pizza, pop and a whole bunch of new friends, excited kids.

One dark night later that year, the Citation, sans rear brakes, rolled down my driveway with a proud new owner who said the e-brake was stopping it just fine. He had seven other Citations, and I suspect the gal accompanying him had eleven cats.

Sam's gone now, too. Cancer got his left lung like a rusted rocker panel. What's left of that night is the memory of Emma the Navigator, like a child of Lourdes, senses on fire, climbing out of the grey cloth seat of the Citation in the blind school parking lot, hugging me, saying, I always wanted to ride in a real sports car.

PLASTIC JESUS

Anybody knew Colby Barlow would realize that buryin' him was going to be a more than a one six-pack job. Now me and Nadine are sitting here on these folding chairs lookin' at the words *Gentle Shepherd Garden* stenciled on the back, and Nadine keeps elbowing me and saying things like, "He'll be back! I know he'll be back."

"Huh?"

She says, "Look up there! He's back from the dead already."

Up there is the front of the Gentle Shepherd Garden Chapel. They got flowers, a CD of an organ playin' *Nearer My God to Thee*, and a giant stained-glass window lit with big florescent tubes, which I know because it's raining outside when we come through the wooden doors. Up front, the funeral director is trying to put Colby in the wall. They got his ashes in a little box but can't fit him in with all them other little boxes. Actually, them boxes they keep people's cree-mains in look a lot like drawers for kitchen cabinets Nadine and I just bought at the Railroad Salvage Mart.

"See, I told you so," says Nadine, "He's still playing jokes on people. That's just like Col." Ain't hard to see where he got it. Plant potatoes, get potatoes. His old man was the best damn cheater on the dirt circuit. Told a tech inspector once, "Look, Elmer, it's my *job* to cheat, and you guys' *job* to catch me." Family spent all winter pissin' on his Chevy frame out behind the garage—couldn't afford no money to acid-dip her. Next spring at Dog Hollow, they had the lightest Street Stock by 40 pounds.

Nadine's the type of person who doesn't like to see anyone be sick or hurt. How do you think we ended up with Colby Barlow in the first place when his old lady, Bev, wouldn't take him in for radiation? Bev's family is some kind of holy sanctified damn old people who don't want to go to a hospital. Nadine told me Col could come live with us. Next, she just got a hospital bed and all that stuff you need and said, "Come on, Col, you can live with us." I said, "Nadine, we got to think about this."

She told me, "We already did, okay?" Then she kissed me.

Last time I saw Colby, I kissed him. I mean, you know how people look when they got cancer? He was lying there naked on our hospital bed with only a sheet over his skinny self. I couldn't help it. It ain't the same as kissing Nadine, mind you, but he was on lots of dope by then, and the doctor told Nadine he wouldn't give Col no more because he might get constipated. Nadine ain't the kind of person who takes fool things lightly. She gave Doc Pangbourne one of her hairy-eyeball stares then told him to get his old butt in gear and rev up this morphine drip to help with the pain. Anyway, I was heading out the door to double-out at the Flyin' A Gas & Go where I worked since high school and the sight of him so sick just caught me, I guess. I thought he'd be gone before I came back, so I kissed him, said, "Sleep, Brother. Rest."

Nadine nudges me again and says, "See..." Up front the maintenance man is there now, and the reverend got beads of sweat on his head, but Colby's box don't want to go nowhere. Besides, the smell of this place is getting to me because it reminds me of the dead guy in the trunk of the Corvette they dragged out of the quarry last year. Funeral places do that to me, ya know?

Col's funeral service was last week, and everybody showed for it. We decorated both front doors of the hearse with his number, 69, and stuck "The Colby Barlow Special" in big letters on the back door where they slid his coffin in. Everybody brought their street rods with big tires, flames painted on them and superchargers stickin' out of the hood including some guys from the Woodward cruise way up in Detroit. People were passing the bottle of tequila around at the church and we all cheered in front of the church when Kerry, the knucklehead that got lucky and won the New Alex demo derby last year, finally knocked the worm down. Just thinking about Colby made you want to do dumb-shit things like that. At McCoy's, people got up and told stories about how crazy we'd all act together and Col would be the looniest. But his mom came from all the way across the state and read an essay he wrote in the fourth grade about car safety that won him an autographed picture of Ralph Nader and the principal signed it, too. After she read it, she tucked it in the coffin under his folded hands.

Col and Bev were married on Halloween. You know, a trick-or-treat wedding, so everybody pitched together and bought four dozen rubbers; we decorated the honeymoon car with them instead of tin cans. When the happy couple came out high from the wedding reception at night, they thought they were balloons. Some expensive balloons! Col just laughed when they got back from the honeymoon, and the next day when Bev was driving the Safe-Sex Camaro to work, the car stopped dead on the expressway and she popped the hood and found three of those white rascals stuffed tight and cozy in the air-intake.

Now, the Reverend Brother Elroy and Jake the janitor are up there with flashlights looking in the hole to see why Colby don't fit, and Nadine tells me now that this is a true sign that Colby is going to be with us a long time, at least in spirit-form. She says her grandmom believes the dead always come back to see if you love them and if you talk to them and pray to them, they stay around. I used to pray when I was little but kinda got over the habit. We learned about saints in C.C.D., but most of them looked like they was on drugs, all pie-eyed, you know. But then there's Francis who talked to animals, so, I guess, that's good for a saint or anybody.

Nadine's got a good job at the Acme Plastics on the river outside of town. She's smart, too. She makes windshields out of plastic for fighter planes like the F 1-11. Sometimes she gets to test 'em by firing chickens out of an air-cannon. Chickens are dead, mind you, but they ain't frozen, and Nadine got hired to fill a quota for government contract work. She says the chickens stimulate sea gulls hitting the cockpits. After splatterin' birds all day, Nadine comes home all philosophical-like about how life has to have a higher purpose.

Things ain't like that at the Flyin' A for me. Guys come down all night in their rollbacks and wait like vultures for calls to come cracklin' over their two-ways about someone broke down. Boys in their pro street cars come over after the cruises, too, and we just sit around till almost sun-up bench racing and talking about Col now and how he could make things funny and stupid and better. But when he was dying, you know, only a couple of people came to see him, and he told me he didn't want to see them either. Well, a few of us got together and played a trick on him. We bought some real good gange—a big bag. I rang our doorbell, and yelled, "Hey, look, all the guys kicked in with a present for you!" He smoked some of it and said, "This is some real good shit." Hell, we figured it was okay for guys to come and see him then because there was nothing he could do to stop them anyway. Still, I noticed there's a lot more people came to the funeral than came to our house to see him when he was still alive, when you didn't have to imagine him talking to you.

Right now, the CD is starting again and they finally got Colby tightened up and torqued down in the *Wall of the Beloved.* Brother Elroy is going to tell us to shake hands and go in peace, and we'll all walk out of here together. I know Nadine won't forget to talk to Colby, but that's Nadine all the way.

Me, I have this picture of us all draining a few Millers around the pool of the Starlite & Starbrite Motel late at night after the Harrisonburg race. It was when Col was sick the first time, and they took his foot then his leg. He was still trying to race, and some fool says, "Hey, Leadfoot, you think your fake foot will float?" Col whips that sucker off, throws it in the pool, then shouts, "Be damned if it don't!" And he falls in the deep end right after it. I'm gonna cut him out of that picture of all of us holding beers and Colby, bird-dog wet, leaning on me waving his leg filled with beer like it's the best trophy in the world then paste him on the dash of my pickup. You best believe it.

Out in the cornfields where the woods got heavy.

Out in the back of my '60 Chevy.

—**Bob Seger**

HAND DANCING

Four cars ahead in creeping heat-haze,
two arms rise from a sunroof
into sight-line
through traffic's glare and glint:
slender, wiggling, snapping hands
clapping in parkway-jammed traffic.

Rhythm and shimmy of hurry up
& wait. Temp gauge tempers boiling over.
Gold baubles on dangles
and finger rings moving
to bottle-necked, stalled steel and concrete
Jersey barriers.
Punch the FM scan, crane
out my window/door to tap the beat
and sight and flight of dancing slitherings.

Aah, sass and flash and forget-me-not
red nails, dancing braceleted
chains now slipping down
hand, wrist, elbow, arm
jam.

I want to know you

along those orange and black striped
traffic barrels.

GRENADE

In the parking lot last night
leaning against the body of your
green Taurus,
I saw you stare at me
then reach your arm up exposing
the side of your body
the curve of your breast
the way a woman does to show she is
vulnerable and powerful both.

Under the sodium vapor lights
you reached back and pulled the
jade hair pin holding your raveled hair,
the hand grenade of your beauty:

Oh, terrorist!
Oh, sweet, sweet assassin.

THREE FOR THE ROAD

Corvette: a highly maneuverable armed escort ship
that is smaller than a destroyer.

SUCH A DEAL

They tell the story of a new Corvette found with a dead man in it
around Forty Acres or Carrie Furnace, I don't remember which.
You can have it for fifteen hundred bucks if you can do some-
thing about the smell of death.

DON'T LET ANYONE TELL YOU YOU CAN'T

Just make sure her bum
doesn't hit the gear shift
if the motor's running.

GATHER YE ROSEBUDS

after Donna Mae

She drove a shocking pink Corvette
hard
when women didn't worry about
a driver's license let alone
454 cubes, posi units and four on the floor.
She drove it hard enough that the bumper
sticker read: CATCH ME & YOU CAN HAVE ME
No one ever bragged about hitting her.
Nobody ever said they could.
I heard, though, she got old
and fat and slow like the rest of us.
The car turned up in the back of a
lot on concrete blocks, and
someone said they saw her
driving a Prius on the Parkway.

MOBILGAS

Dear Mr. Edward Hopper,

Enclosed is a ten-dollar bill in reparation for gasoline my friend and I borrowed from your gas station ten years ago. Since fuel was only seventeen cents a gallon back in 1931, this payment should cover the cost plus interest. I hope you don't remember this shameful action on our part.

We were on our way to Chillicothe, Ohio to meet girls at a grange dance. Your phone in the station rang and Wally, my friend, volunteered to pump by hand. You took so long. I hope it wasn't bad news. We finished topping-up the tank of the model A and it seemed like we waited an eternity. The girls were waiting for us, too. We decided to leave and pay you on the way back. We never stopped.

Last evening, I was driving by your newly remodeled place in my Ford station wagon with my wife. Yes, Millie from the dance and our three kids. The Ford is green with wood trim, the latest thing. Life has been good to me, Mr. Hopper. Three kids a beautiful wife and a new car with a V8 engine.

I want to confide to you, we *should* have danced all night. Long story short, as Millie's dad said, "The baby was right on time; the wedding was eight months late." That day your gasoline helped changed my life. I never put anything but Mobil in the station wagon's tank.

Sincerely,

Robert Wheatfield

P.S. Your new gas pumps with the lighted glass bowls on the top look like heads. You were standing in front of one and writing something down. Millie said you looked so intent like you were asking a girl to dance and signing her dance card. I promise we shall stop next time, and I'll introduce you to my family and the new baby that's on the way, too.

NOT HAVING ENOUGH

of you,
I circle the airport runway.
Dead ahead, tiny planes shimmer
in the explosive heat of takeoff.
Lights blaze,
shake grow, then lift
silver underbellies above
my windshield,

but I miss the logo
of your cheap Jet Train plane,
pull out to circle
home. Then, there above the terminal
the DC9 lifts black & gold
into the Pittsburgh sun.
My car is the fast arc of road
wanting to cross under your flight.
We play tag: curved lines
of our distant shadows in sync.

In terminal traffic,
I lose sight of you.

There is only sun,
now clouds and on the highway home, I look one last time
northeast, above the treeline,
toward New York.

MEMORIAL DAY, OHIO

I

Over the crest of Ohio 7,
Morrison's in the death rattle
of "L.A. Woman". You're
in the crosshairs of a radar gun.
Ease over to the berm,
stupid grin,
kill the radio; the Bear's
polite & happy you're paying
for excesses.
Proceed with caution minus 5
till 7 turns to 30 at Lisbon.
Throttle up to 70, then slow again
for horse trailers and orange farm tractors.

II

Rain is the blurred litany of
small towns and wiper blades:
Kensington, East Rochester,
Minerva, Robertsville—
flags and buntings,
flowers and football teams.
This, the bored seduction
of gingerbread porches,
the pulchritude of contented cows

in a drizzle.
Remember crepe paper
red, white, blue
woven in and out of spokes
on a second-hand bike
for Decoration Day?

III

In a gas station beyond East Canton,
the clerk at the register
is crisp as home-farm lettuce
in BP Greens.
She sells cigarettes, coffee, ice cream,
motor oil in black plastic bottles.
Discuss the rain,
dark hair and a shadow across the
arc of her upper lip. She's plump and
wants to fish when she's done at four
if the rain clears.
Later, on the interstate, you'll see
her face
in the slipstream of a passing semi
and wonder how it would feel
to make love to her
if the rain hadn't stopped by
four o'clock in Ohio.

WRECKAGE

Her smell is still on you, but she is two hundred miles away now. Her warm eyes, how the wisp of her hair kept falling down the side of her face as she read you the dinner specials, the way she touched the tip of the pencil to her lips before she wrote your order. You left her this morning before she awoke. You thought about leaving a note or something, but what can you say to someone needier than you? You told her you were in construction, that you owned an HVAC company. You knew the real college professor would never do. Later that night after it was over, she showed you pictures of her son, maybe ten years younger than your daughter. Why wasn't she with her son? She chose to spend the night in a motel with a stranger she met at the restaurant instead. You told her you just dropped your daughter off at college. That much was true.

Three hundred miles beyond the restaurant where you met the waitress last evening, your daughter is spending the first full day of her own life, growing up, away from you. You ached at how young and brave Amanda looked carrying things from the Jeep Cherokee up to the room in the women's dorm. But, of course, it was a women's dorm; they all were! You chide yourself for forgetting this was the girl's college she wanted to attend way back since the Stone Age of her junior high school days. You both laugh, standing at the car door resting after struggling with her belongings that seemed to say she was ready to for a lifetime instead of nine months. "Now don't come back home at Christmas a flaming feminist or, my God, an Eastern liberal. Wait at least until you are a sophomore!"

You've abandoned your daughter with a lame joke and a weak smile. She is all you have now, along with a note that her mother, your wife, left you both six months ago. You are driving back to the midwestern college where you teach history and to nothingness. Two hundred miles more to home. The morning sun, bright and low behind you, is reflecting in the rearview mirror. Fall is coming, the lengthening shadows and the sun low in the morning's eastern sky. Before this, you loved the passing of the seasons. Now you are afraid if you look up to the mirror, you might see in the reflection of the woman you were with last night whose last name you can't recall, or you'll see Mandy when she is as old as the waitress. Or you might look up to see your wife and think again of the note she left for the both of you that explains everything or nothing and you know she is never coming back the way you are never going back to last night's diner.

Three miles up ahead there will be an accident. It is not your crash but another car coming toward you blinded by that sun in your rearview mirror. You will see the car swerve away from your lane to the far side of the four-lane and up the steep embankment climbing, but not quite over the top of the hill like a midget car in a kiddy circus full of clowns. It will pause, seem to gain balance and composure then begin sliding backwards. The fuel tank will rupture and the bumper will dig into the dirt, flipping the car end-over on its roof. At that instant, you stop directly across the road from the car sliding on its collapsed roof, its inhabitants scrambling half in and half out of the wreck, reborn into terror, imagining the sound of a siren coming from somewhere. You later recall a woman getting out of her pickup truck, cell phone in hand, ready to light flares. You'll get out of your car but won't do anything more heroic or cowardly than anyone else this morning. Still, it will be vouchsafed to you at some future date that you must choose to crawl out of the crushed and glittering womb of your own wreck as it slides backwards down the embankment which your life has lately become.

Someday your life will pass before you.

It had better be interesting.

—Oscar Wilde

INTERACTIVE MEMORY BLITZ

Dear Reader, did you think we'd drive all this way without you taking a turn at the wheel? *You have ten minutes to list the ten most memorable rides you have ever taken.* No title needed. Spelling doesn't count. No particular order.

Ready. Set…

What! Give you some examples?

I'll spot you my five. Please pay attention!

1. Taking Charlotte to the hospital for the birth of our sons, Kevin and Eric.

2. The kid with eyes big as hubcaps. The kid who just ran in front of your van beside Colfax Elementary. The SCHOOL ZONE 15 mph sign. Somehow, today you knew better & cut it to 5. The best miss of your life? Anticipation. Good for ketchup and driving in school zones.

3. A car cruze (think big-engined, American muscle cars). You walk away to peruse the "tangerine, metalflake streamlined babies," quote Tom Wolfe. When you come back there is a young man in a wheelchair looking at your car. He knows all about your Healey 3000. Says he was injured in a crash when a friend was showing off speeding. Bob will be wheelchair-bound for the rest of his life. Now dad transports him to car events. He'd like to see the 3000 race at the PVGP next summer but he has been getting weaker & weaker…

4. I flip my grandson the keys to the Audi TT. "Let me show you how to drive a stick (six speed at that)." Start out on a slight downgrade, be patient, gradually go to a level road, be patient then try a slight uphill. Be real patient.

My dad never taught me to drive. My friends, T.J. and Pokey, did. After the first try with my father, I just didn't want to listen to the word *clutch* said in anger over and over. I never asked again. Hey, the man was a good dad. I know when I get out of the Audi and point skyward I'll silently say: *See, Dad, that's how it is done*, he'll get it now.

(You were, Dear Reader, expecting hair-on-fire, wild to be wreckage, drive-it-like-you-stole-it examples, correct?)

5. Did you ever get air under all four wheels? Consider the jump at Weatherly Hillclimb. Launch just right at Weatherly and the windshield becomes blue sky and the green leaves on Pennsylvania trees. Keep your wheels straight on touchdown. If not, you may hit the boulder on the far side of the road. They, the other drivers, will name the boulder after you but only for that day.

Your turn.

1.

2.

3.

4.

5.

6.

7.

8.

9.

10.

FIND A MEDIUM-SIZE OPOSSUM

Skin, cut, clean.
It is usually best to prepare
the *mire poix* before hand. You
may substitute shallots for onions.
Choose an agreeable white
(pinot grigio, perhaps), add half
cup and a quarter stick of butter,
double wrap aluminum foil,
double lock the seams.

Remove the heat shield from
the exhaust manifold (if present).
Place the bolts in a baggie
and store all in the trunk. (Upon
reassembly, consider coating
bolt threads with anti-seize
to facilitate future removal.)

Place the opossum on the manifold
for one hundred fifty miles.
If the engine is turbocharged,
cut the mileage by about one third.

THE WOMEN OF BRICK ALLEY

One side of the road falls off into deep shadows.
It is night on the hill in East McKeesport.
Your Oldsmobile dies near the car wash.
A man walks up, insists on helping,
shoving your car away from the lights
toward the darkness.
You argue. He grabs your arm.

Then suddenly, two women appear.
He takes off.

The short woman with the two gold hoops
 in her ear says, "It's the alternator."
The other woman, staring at the hood
seems to agree. They stay till
you call a friend to come pick you up.
Next day, Zip says, "You want a new or rebuilt alternator?"

Angels. You say it again: *Angels,*

but you remember then
after the cops closed down Brick Alley,
the women of McKeesport moved up Route 148
to East McKeesport, began retraining,
studying anything they could get their blessed hands on
about the nature of alternating current.

LAST RIDE

> *I don't want a plain box*
> *I want a sarcophagus.*
>
> —Sylvia Plath

Forget the sarcophagus,
Sylvia baby.
I need a pickup truck—
Lincoln pearlescent white
pulled by six champagne Arabians
black shakos dancing,
tires big as a Prius
and a rope ladder to get in.

Lay me out like Donna Mae, her
Corvette pink with Marilyn
air-brushed across the hood.
A Corvette cortège followed like rabid dogs
carbon paw prints to the banks of the Lethe,
howling all the way.

When some sweet sales gal whispers, *And*
it has an unlimited mileage warranty—
Tell 'er, *But I don't…*
Just a little pick'em-up to make
Texas schoolgirls in cowboy boots
squeal, and NASCAR mamas
vote two thumbs up.

Order up an engine-turned dash,
a plastic leather steering wheel, a power plant
called Cummins, Hemi or Power-Stroke.
Stacks risin' from the box,
amber clearance lamps, a serious lift-kit with
blue neon under the running boards.
I need Roseanne Cash breathing *Black Cadillac*
then Lynyrd Skynyrd or Willie for intermission.
Goin' gently into that good night?
I don't think so.

SWING LOW

for Rege

Swing low sweet blanket of suds.
 Wash my body in your bubbles.
      Rinse my sins into your gutter.

I believe you're not responsible
   for ornaments and mirrors.
Oh, Lord may your sprays spray,
      (I'll retract my antenna)
your lights blink:

      HOT WAX   HOT WAX

      Let the Jordan of your waters
cleanse salt-sinned undercarriage.
   Bring the sweet tree palm
      gyrating leaves of love
            &
flap crud from fouled panels of my chariot.
   Spit-shine the chrome & sparkle
      my windows. Let me see that—
            wait, wait—

There's a dripdrop on my rapture.

Down, down my windshield.

      Why you got that sucker!
   Shimmy, shimmy, hubba, hubba cap hosanna.

Pass the tip jar, please.

PARKWAY JAM

(OR THE GREAT GEOLOGICAL BOOGIE)

Stuck in traffic?
    Parkway jammed, Mon Warf flooded,
       pot-holes looming, bridges bowing, tempers rising:
No wonder you can't get there from here!

Welcome to the great geological dance.
The boogie started ages before we arrived,
    before the parkway
        orange plastic barrels
           jersey barriers (& Jersey, for that matter).

Way before written language:
YIELD
  DETOUR
    SLOW—my mommy works here.

Back then the Monongahela backed up from an Ice Age chill.
Bloomfield, Millvale, Edgewood-Swissvale & Oakland's all
awash.
That giant glacier shuffling south
stoppered the flow at Monaca, backed up, when it popped
out poured the Ohio south & west 'stead of north to Erie's basin.

Saddle up your favorite mastodon.
Let's call him Ally-Oop. Ride up to Mount Washington,
let him slurp from Glacial Lake Monongahela.

Twenty thousand years,
    lots of language over the dam-
        tons of geological shimmy,
            tectonics plates a-shifting,
                tempers & temperatures rising.

Turn up your imagination.

Tap your feet to the Parkway Jam!
Earth dance, slow, silent music
boogying (that great rhythm) eons down the road.

FAMOUS BELLYBUTTONS I HAVE KNOWN

Tanya

See this fuzz?
Yeah.
Every time we make love, I'll give you some.

Hope I get enough to make a pillow, a mattress.

We'll see.

Piercing

The first time he saw her with her navel exposed, a hoop spar-
kling, it turned his stomach.

The second time, yeah, he got it: The ancient story made sexy
and perverse; nothing new here.

The third time he figured he might attach a gold chain to the hoop
and pull her around, but who'd want someone that stupid, vain
and innocent following you.

Moral

His studio was on a hill at the bend of the road. The sculptor took
damaged, rotten and nuisance trees from the town and gave them

life as art—tables, torso sculptures, wall hangings, smoothed, glossed, loved once again. One day a car towing a U-Haul trailer came past and the trailer uncoupled. The car kept going; the trailer rolled at a tangent to the bend. He was standing outside of his studio. The tongue of the trailer impaled the sculptor.

Mom

What's this, Mom?

It's your bellybutton.
Where's it come from?
Me.
Then we're connected?
Yep.
I love you.

Dad

What's this, Dad?
Don't touch that!
What is it?
Your bellybutton, don't mess with it.
What'll happen?
It holds you together;
you don't want your bum to fall off, do you?

Oh!

OCCAM'S CHICKEN

Last night I saw a lady give a chicken a bath on television. She washed the chicken under its wing pits and put a little red diaper on it and even rode the chicken around in her convertible in a ritzy neighborhood sitting in a baby seat with a seatbelt. This was no ordinary chicken, I gather, but a blue-blood bird with a pedigree and papers and white fluffy feathers. The lady hugged the chicken then took it for a swim in her outdoor pool, and I have to admit, I think the woman was naked, at least from the waist up. It was a big swimming pool with a palm tree at one end, and the only thing I wonder is, what does that chicken have that I don't.

THE CHICKEN, THE ROAD, THE WIDOW

Okay, I admit you may think it's a little strange. As chickens go, I never thought of myself as anything special and never thought too much about fate, karma—call it what you want—until a certain red convertible came roaring down the road past Yarnick's Poultry Farm and into my life. Before that, life was hunt and peck, peck and hunt, a clean coop and a good perch was all I thought I needed...

That one day, though, I was crossing the road on a bet, a dare. Wham-o! I'm ass-over-tin-cups into the ditch on the other side. Turns out, it's her, Marlene. She rushes over to the ditch, blonde with tears in her hazel eyes. She scoops me up. Still, I'm in bad shape; she tries for weeks to nurse me back. As I heal, we grow closer. She starts to call me Chick-Chick, but only when we are alone. In front of Darcy and her other friends, I'm Sidney. I cluck Mar-Mar sweet and low, letting the alliteration swirl around my beak before it reaches her ears. I notice she has a slight up-turn at the end of her nose. So what, nobody's perfect. Our shyness is beautiful.

She tells me Milton, her husband, was killed by a runaway Steinway, I don't know all the facts but it flattened him—it did, I know that. Death does strange things to loved ones. Darcy, her friend, needed six parrots to forget about her hubby when he bought the farm (if you'll excuse the cliché). I have to hold my tongue about the six parrots.

My limp grows less noticeable as the weeks pass. I have to face the fact, though, it will be with me for the rest of my life. Finally, I am able to flap up onto the green Amazon parrot's perch that Darcy gave her. I get the run of the house in a little red diaper with Velcro flaps that look striking against my white plumage.

I never was a big cable TV fan and I'm used to her going away, but she switches on Animal Planet to keep me company. It's way too much Darwin and "the bloody tooth and claw" for my stomach. I won't hurt her feelings for anything, though. What I like is the travel channels and Charlie Rose but only when he is having a good night. Later on in the summer when I'm strong enough, we go out for rides in her Mustang. She has a baby seat and buckles me in. One evening at the Dairy Queen, a pickup truck with two Rottweilers parks beside us. I never saw such a pair of drooling, three-time losers in my young life. It's not my SwirlCurl top cone they're slobbering at, and I'd love to flip them the bird but, I don't make eye contact till we're pulling the hell out of the parking lot.

About two weeks after the dog scare, Marlene's in the kitchen with her friends. I shift my weight to the edge of the perch, lean toward the kitchen, tune out the TV. "You should do it," they all agree. Then Darcy leans forward, her voice sounding like a door chime. "Hon-ee, Mr. Right, Mr. Right-Now, you can't tell the difference till you get up close and personal. Someone needs to find a guy to dampen her panties." Marlene's face reddens. "What are you waiting for?" They all like eHarmony or match.com. The next few months I meet a steady stream of Fox-News loving, channel surfing, subtle as a bug-zapper characters. With this parade of sad comb-overs I don't get a chance to watch any of my favorite cable shows.

Hey, Mar-Mar's a rich widow in a convertible, what's not to like? But I have nagging doubts she is not telling these guys about me before the first date. I have to live with that one. Sure, I miss everybody at the coop, the simple life, the smell of chicken feed and grass, but now, this is my life—our life. Luckily, most of these losers don't get to first base. That is, till I start hearing the name "Brad" when she is on the phone with Darcy. "Brad this, Brad that." It gets under my feathers. The guy's a different kind of comb-over. Brings candy, flowers, writes her little poems. I know enough to be worried. Where are Rottweilers when you need 'em?

One night, Bradley shows up at our front door with a bottle of pinot grigio. The two of them plop down to watch TMC, *Rear Window*, one of my favorites. Pretty soon they're kissing. They only come up for air when Jimmy Stewart falls out of the window. Movie ends, and Fred and Ginger are up next. Marlene and Knucklehead start to dance right in front of me. Right, I'm jealous. But I try to let it pass. I notice his pupils are dilating. All of a sudden, he dances her toward the hallway and they disappear. I'm like, "Excuse me for breathing." I flip channels to keep my mind off what's going on. After a few minutes, I hear a scream. Ignoring my gimpy leg, I hop off the perch, flap down the hallway which is strewn with their clothing. As I round the corner to her bedroom, I hear her shout, "Oh, God! Oh, God!" He's naked on top of her. Then, rightly or wrongly, I assume I've caught the guy *in flagrante dilecto,* so I hop on his keister clamping tight as I can with my claws and start beaking his cheek. He yowls, knocks me away with a back-hand, rolls over and falls off the bed onto the new Berber rug. I hop up on the nightstand with hubby's picture and their wedding rings still side by side. He comes after me like Colonel Sanders, so I'm up on the mahogany dresser where he lunges at me. It's flap-hop-step, flap-hop-step to the opposite side of the bedroom. Hairy Butt starts around the bed but trips over her exercycle and slams his shin. He's hopping around on one foot now holding his other and I notice his schwanz, which, an instant ago was unusually large, looks like a worm in a patch of grass. I hear Marlene giggling. Then she starts to laugh. He glares at her and I boogie out of the room and down the narrow hallway, past the living room TV (Hitler is invading Russia for the third time this month), down the steps of the split-level and perch up on the antlers of the deer head above the pool table in the family room. I try to look calm. Above me, voices, shouting. A door slams. It's quiet for a few minutes then footsteps. The front door opens then slams shut. A car starts and drives away…

The house quiets again and I close my eyes but sleep fitfully. I move like a zombie from dream to waking and back. In one dream Vanna White says, "Sidney, Precious, which of the three doors will you pick tonight?" I know the Georgia Chicken Growers Association is behind the green door waiting for me to deliver a speech. Behind the second, Marlene and the Mustang convertible, but I'm lying in the dirt road: the license plate, the bumper, the dual exhausts throbbing down the road, her blonde head of hair getting smaller till she power-slides the car around a dusty bend and heads towards the grain elevator in town. A gang of white leghorns are on the farm side of the road pointing and yukking it up, screaming, "You lost! You lost!" I go for the third door but wake at the sound of the creaking hinge.

Next morning, I'm on the perch deep in thought about the *Sturm und Drang* of love when I hear Marlene laugh. She's on the phone with Darcey Six Parrots telling her the story of her date and laughing as she tells it. But she's not trying to cover her mouth like she did up in the bedroom. She's laughing so hard, she starts to cry. I don't realize it till right then, but I guess Bradley does look pretty funny with a chicken clamped on his rear.

After Mar-Mar hangs up, she comes over to me, and I know everything's kosher between us. She picks up the remote, turns off Animal Planet, says with a big smile, "Chick-Chick, Chick-Chick. Does widdle Sidney want to 'wim in mommy's pool?" I hop up on her hand being careful not to scratch her. We walk over to the French doors and out into the flower garden. She lets the bathrobe slip from her shoulders and unhooks the top of her bikini. It drops onto the Delft blue tile-edge of the swimming pool. I hop back on her hand and she wades into the shallow water. At the far end of the pool, the morning sun casts a shadow from the Costa Rican palm. "Yes," I think to myself, "Hell, yes, widdle Sidney does want to 'wim in mommy's pool."

A car is a creature that lives with its own emotions and its own heart. You have to understand and love it accordingly.

—Juan Manuel Fangio

CLICK

for Kevin

That knuckle-busting winter
the creeper slid on gray grease cold,
coffee cups of high-test
warming on the Kerosun.
The Saturday's whorl of thumbprint
bookmark *Haynes Manual,*
quick index for engine ills.

Odometer pushing ninety-seven thou.
Speedo stooped at zero. Still,
we hauled her home—
peach baskets full of
pipe-dream projects.

Soon, Christmas jewelry fool's gold
glittering brass trunnion
beneath the rusting ball joints.

Well, this spring she come easing
down (click, click),
rust and crud among new glitter
from her jack-stand perch.

Shutter, putter, making/breaking for
the light of day

beyond the green garage door:
carb sputter, valve clatter, clutch judder.

Whiff us a blue kiss of oil-rich smoke,
and how our grill-wide grins. The proud.
The emblem. The rusty success.

BREAKFAST

Between fingers burnt and scarred from
jumpstarting the souls of reluctant trucks
all week, eggs broke with the sounds
of the Host in the priest's hands.
Those Sunday mornings when
he drove us home from church,
we cajoled my father to cook.

Small suns rose into a world
of sizzling grease. He turned when done
toward the ringing silverware,
the whiteness of his apron brocaded
egg gold and ketchup red.
The old man served each of his flock,
daughters and sons with the words,
Come on, kid, you can't stand on one foot.
Take more!

We were fully nourished in a faith
solid as the straight-eight engine in that Buick,
joyous as the long-tooth gleam of its grill
cooling at the curb, back from a trip
to Saint Henry's Church.

SHANKSVILLE, FLIGHT 93

About this the old masters are wrong.
There are no miracles,
no mythical boy plunging
headlong into the ocean. Only the wind
cartwheeling pages of the book
till I clamp them with scarred thumbs.
And beyond the pale of wreaths,
dolls and flowers, candles and signs so full
the kid with dreadlocks writes
to the dead and living on the flag's pole,
beyond the couple on the chopper
and the delivery man on break, you
will stand on bare earth.
Face the fence a quarter mile away
at the point of impact
and read into the wind:
Give not up thy heart to sadness
But drive it from thee,
For there is no returning
And thou shalt do them no good...

And the wind bears no witness
for me.

II

Bruegel could have painted here
in Western Pennsylvania where the earth moves
like my grandmother shaking out her apron

into the rhythm of fields and distance, and
mist rises from low runs in this season.
He would have known the yellow school bus driver,
her cowboy boots and string-back driving gloves,
the CAT operator climbing down from his dozer,
the old-timers at the station giving
directions, *You tell 'em, Dennis!*

Soon darkness will come
in this season of dying.
The earth, tilting on her axis,
lengthens shadows
and Bruegel will put down his pallet
clean his brushes and pack a pipe
to mix with the smell of windfall apples.

III

The tanker glistens like a fuselage,
double yellow reflecting
in its convex end—
a line of tracer bullets.
Driving along the top of the ridge,
you want to mash the accelerator,
pull into the oncoming lane, let the
Mustang be distorted in the flanks
of the Somerset Oil Company semi.

Back off;
they're not going anywhere.

The rig turns off right.
You serpentine through

a stand of dark pines,
exit into the desert strip-mine landscape:
Property of DIAMOND T COAL CO.
Turn off two-way radios when blasting
over the north ridge horizon
the crane boom, huge flag,
then a trail of dust
more flags. The road veers off mid-slope.
The memorial!

Go there.

Heading home, take the road from Friedens
like the old-timers tell you.
Around the curve
Shanksville's last gas station,
no pumps,
but still the shield above,
red and white and blue.
The torch of freedom
balanced on the arch of AMOCO.

REST STOP, I-80

Open the car door to a
week of heat. Hillside dry
hay color, and

the smell of burning,
not grass nor grass but
something odd,

herb-like—
incense?
Up behind the visitor's center,

low shade trees.
Patches of green
under one tree. A

man sits cross-legged.
Smoke rising in front.
You watch awhile.

Smoke dies.
The man rises,
folds the rug.

A breeze from
Pennsylvania woods
signals evening.

He will walk down
past your picnic bench,
a dark eagle feather in his hand.

He nods,
you both smile. He will cross the black-river
asphalt of parking lot,
check load binders, climb up
into the cab of the Western Star.

Move into the press of the interstate
away from you both,
this stilled moment.

DRIVE-BY

Westmoreland was a couple of clicks above Siagon.
The Mamas and Papas were California dreaming, and
we were here, West By God Virginia, to teach kids of these hills.
Part of LBJ's Great Society.

Classes in Huntington a flood-plane between the Ohio and
Appalachia's spine. Rookie teachers for National Teacher Corps
classes, parties, singing seminars, Harry Cawdill's *Night Comes
to the Cumberlands* then traversing hills and switchbacks
toward Red Mud Ridge and beyond.

That summer she and I were just friends, honest, crossing one of
Huntington's college streets when somebody, say, just a kid in a
passing car shot a "Nigger Lover" out the window at me. The
brass shell casing hot, glittering like a Third Eye in the gutter by
our feet or maybe I just imagine that part now.

What I don't imagine after all these years is the way she looked
up at me.
That look (high cheekbones, Cherokee, she thought)
fear, admiration, derision, now you know,
everything
that boy in the car speeding away from us may have felt, also.

I looked away from her, down the street,

checked for more traffic then she and I crossed together.

TALKING SMACK TO THE DEAD

Listen to me, brother, it was a dumb-shit
    thing to do. Hear me? Nobody believed
you went in your sleep.
    Too full of life & cool & class
and quick lap times. Full-throttle adrenalin,
    wrapped in a shy smile, hand out to help,
never talked trash behind someone's back. But you
    talked driving & everyone shook their head
in the same way.

    Nobody. Believed. It.

Ex-triathlete turned driver & national champion,
    I'd spend all day to get within two seconds of you
& gladly spend another to trade for a second
    more. No. When you pulled off on the side of the interstate
you dropped the checker, you stopped the timer
    and your heart on your own.

You reached into the glove compartment and this isn't lost
    on any of us:
piston
    bullet
        slug
            barrel
                cylinder
                    chamber
                      velocity
                        smoke.

Raff, I can see you cresting *Madness,* your ride a rat
   with tennis shoes out of the corners, balls-out
down the straight.
   The Supra beautiful as a woman whispering, *Yes.*
Was she your Dark Angel?

 The rap: we didn't know you. But, man,
it was you who didn't know you. A lost love,
   a job, talent slowing. That's not
your *memento mori.* That's not
   what we saw in you.

LITTLE BASTARD

Sunlight intensifies the scene as if
lit by Fresnel spots.
He is centered with his '50s Existential
scowl. Three gas pumps
(red, square-headed),
a Ford station wagon, the blue of the sky
ground the photo.

Little Bastard is gassed and waiting
as he slips on string-back driving gloves.
The white tee, jeans,
a cigarette precariously balanced
on his lip, complete the picture.

Eden, Rebel, Giant are behind him,
out of the frame. Now a director
might ask him to vault one-handed
over the low door of the Porsche
Spyder into the red leather cockpit
for a Le Mans start like Rodriguez
did at Sebring.

Up ahead the director will caution
about a left turn across traffic
toward the road race near Salinas,
autumn sun in an oncoming driver's eyes.

Eternity.

WHAT HE REMEMBERS

for D. S.

Just beyond number 5 flagging station the road bends a little to the left then right before it sweeps into the fast left-hander. You come into that jog faster than expected, swing the car back to the right, barely holding on then brake too hard for the turn. The rear tires lock up on the down-shift spinning the car off the road scattering hay bales put there to protect from the rural mailbox. But the box tears open the fuel tank under the red and white Lola's aluminum skin. Wheels on the right-side slide then hook in the drainage ditch launching the race car into a barrel-roll. Air borne, upside down you think, *So this is how it ends.*

You were there in the pits that morning as the sun came over the pines. There was nothing you didn't love about racing these hillclimbs in the powerful cars of the unlimited class. You wanted to be first to the hill in the morning, dew so thick it would soak through your shoes as you fiddled to get the car ready for the day's competition. There was the snick, snick of throttle plates on the Weber carbs, the smell of Castrol and racing fuel, the cold cough and sputter of air intakes as the Traco-Chevrolet engine cleared itself and warmed to life. When the idle settled, you smiled, thought again of Fangio's words, "A car is like a creature that lives with its own emotions and its own heart. You have to understand and love it accordingly." The great Formula I driver remained your favorite throughout your life.

After the car flips, it rolls twice and comes to rest on its wheels. You are shaken by the impact, barely conscious, and try to find your harness and belt buckle. Then suddenly it happens. You become conscious of everything that is going on but unafraid, unhurried and detached at the same time. Beyond the necessity of the situation, you sense the sensual beauty of it all, the sharp crack, the explosion of gasoline then oil as the dry-sump tank ignites in the cockpit beside you. There is the orange curtain of flame and your total disconnect from the happenings. You sense flaming Nomex gloves in front of you; they seem yours. They must be yours, and you have perfect thought-control of these disembodied hands as they float out of the flames and across your field of vision in a slow deliberate arc to release the harness on the second try. You see yourself crawling from the burning wreck, your driver suit in flames. You stand outside of the scene as in a lucent dream and know precisely what you will do next: as a combat fighter pilot in Korea years before, you were taught to clear the danger then dive and roll to smother flaming clothing. Beyond the white shroud that covers you, voices call now. "Where am I? What is it? What are they saying?"

When the chemical fog clears, you see the flared nozzles of fire extinguishers aimed at you then corner-workers from Turn 5 standing over you. In the background, others battle the burning field and the house that caught fire just beyond the corner.

Witnesses that lined the hillclimb course from the start line up said there was dust rising at the berm on each side of the road from huge Goodyear slicks as the T70 Lola Chevrolet wove up the twisting road, straightening it, gaining speed at an alarming rate. At the inquest, the wreck was ruled *a racing incident* with no negligence involved. The spectators injured with flaming debris at Turn 1 were released from the hospital several days afterward. The house which caught fire in the field was extinguished by the corner-workers. The monster Lola became a charred and melted toy. Later, you would haul her home.

There was always a strangeness about this place. When it rained on summer evenings, you have seen mist come off the mountain like a sheer dress drops from a woman's shoulders. On a clear day, from the crest of the hill, the river and towns are visible along the valley almost to New York State. Beyond the finish line over the crest, there is an overgrown monument marking the spot where three Revolutionary War soldiers were speared, stabbed and scalped by Indians. Now, near the start line, there are remains of miners' houses, abandoned because of cave-ins, miner's deaths and stinking sinkholes of mine subsidence.

Everyone knew this hill was raced since the beginning of the last century, first by automakers like Louis Chevrolet to sell cars that were strong and fast on the hill and by famous drivers like Rene Dreyfus the WWI flying ace. The sixty-second mark was only bested, finally, at the end of the 1950s by Carroll Shelby, a driver of international reputation. Today is the day for you and the monster T70 to break the fifty-second mark, you felt.

As you grow older, you begin to understand part of what happened on the hill that day and are not afraid to tell people. You want others to understand your responsibility for the accident. Your family and children should know you are a just and honest and hard-working man; you wish the injuries sustained by the spectators could be your own. That morning long ago in the paddock at the hillclimb, you knew you could set a new record well below the minute mark with the T70. Now, by your own judgment because of your driving, you lost the right to race that hill ever again. The remains of the Lola will sit, covered like a shroud, in your garage for the rest of your life, but driving is your life; you know that. You will don your Nomex, your balaclava, the helmet and gloves again and set several records on other hills. What you remember, though, what you dream about for the rest of your life are flaming gloved hands, burning in front of you. Ethereal. Your hands and yet not your hands.

BELT IN   SHUT UP   HANG ON

—Instructions on the dash of a race car

CLARK'S LOTUS GRABBING AIR

I

How little you know of us,
writing only precious truth
and not fact.
Sometimes the road does stretch out forever
like dust rose behind your pickup on
the dirt road near Ruffner's Curve,
or Havana 1957:
the sky, the sea melting,
and Fangio's three-litre Maserati drifts
the esses onto the Malecon,
later Jimmy Clark's Lotus grabbing air
over the jump at Nurburgring.

II

Poem Whore,
only interested in our death.
This is the double-clutch downshift
into *Oh Shit*. The chassis settles like
Coltrane's fingered keys on *Naima*.
I kiss the apex,
drift out to the edge. Poet,
you grow smaller in my mirrors.

IN THE WAITING ROOM OF THE SPEEDY MUFFFLER KING

Ashtrays full of crushed butts, and
the man in scrub blues glides
on soft soles, speaks in hushed tones:
"See here where cancer has eaten her away."
He has studied mortuary science.

You'll do anything to save her.

You notice the patch on his blue shirt,
white with red letters, says "Ted."

THE COMPLETELY UNHERALDED JUMPING FROG OF CALAVERAS COUNTY

From the sweet
susurrus of the crickets
by the redwood,
down the wooded path,
even across the silver
river of moonlight highway,
Taylor, the little frog, thought
the world was his lily pad.

Mummzie neglected to mention
the double-clutchin',
motherfuckin' Peterbilt
called *Francis the Toad Stomper*
pulling out at a loading dock, westbound,
from Chicago.

SONNET FOR THE BOYS IN THE HOMEWOOD CEMETERY

Over the hill from mausoleums that spell
Mellon and Frick and Hillman, they unload
beer from a hearse called The Grim Sleeper.
Jacked-up, punched-out, supercharged,
Summit Racing catalog's answer to immortality.
While the night watchman's arthritic fingers
search the night sky for the Pirates game
from the coast, his shepherd snores in a
sliver of light from the gatehouse door. Hey, man,
what the hell; Death has a sense of humor, too.

I once tried to give her a hotfoot. But that
was when I was twenty. Someday she'll chuck us all
under the chin as she lays us in that cool lawn gently
and sighs, "Boys will be boys."

INTERVIEW WITH THE BACK-UP GIRL

My man was a drag slick, a wheelstand,
a hundred miles an hour
backwards down the strip. He was
P. T. Barnum in a nitro burning Funny Car.
I was his back-up girl.

Like the Hammers of Hell
he left the burn-out box—
smoke, flames, thunder.
Ever smell nitromethane?
I strode out of the smoke,
legs long enough to make a model cry.
Cut-off jeans (my Daisy Maes I called 'em!),
a halter top holdin' my lovelies up.
Hands on my hips, legs apart,
I stared down that thousand horse-power
Funny Car. I was his back-up girl.

All cheers, all eyes on me. He,
caged inside, Nomex, boots, gloves,
breathing cans on a mask. Nitro sears
the lungs with a yellow flame.

I signaled *Reverse*
His praying mantis, goggled eyes
on me. All eyes on me:

 A little Left.

No, that's Right, dummy.
You got it. Hold it straight now.
   Back
       Back
          Back
The fist in the air was mine.
He stopped behind the line.
I went down on one knee,
thrust the other leg out.
All eyes on me.
(Girls, you know what I mean.)
No oil, fuel or fire.
Thumbs up.

The Snake, the Mongoose, Big Daddy-
we raced 'em all.
People loved the circus. Just
glad I didn't pack his 'chute
in Pomona that day.

And, yes, when he found me
I was eighteen, beautiful,
in a nowhere Pennsylvania town.
Get in, he said—we hooked
like drag slicks on the strip,
a jungle-rumble in the hay.
What a ride. I'm glad
I didn't pack his 'chute that day.
But he was no fool. Never
said, *I want to die behind the wheel.*
No dumb-shit stuff like that.
We were always a jungle-rumble in the hay.

At the funeral chapel,
(Sure, we understand.
You want to be alone with him,
one more time.) when our friends left,

I opened the urn,
touched him to my
tongue. We still burn
yellow in the afternoon sun.

KEY WEST: FEBRUARY

Evening fans out against the sky
iridescent as a gamecock's feathers, and
you are the white cat dancing
en pointe in Mallory square,
I, the dog in dark glasses
who waits on the Harley for hand-outs.
Tourists come, laugh, snap shutters,
cast dollars in up-turned hats.
Their nights are crisp white linen,
amaretto-lacquered lips in staterooms
of the *Royal Sovereign*, but

our night comes on like a black-flack fighter.
We straddle the throb of a V-twin,
two-up, cruise back streets,
lights veining alleys past clapboard
chapels while white-gloved Black women
sing, "Lord Make Me Your Vessel,"
and fingers splay above our Tarot
like the mangrove root.
Over these streets, Hemingway catwalked away
from Pauline toward wife three,
and the smell of deep-fried black-eyed peas
tumbles from windows
to pillows of bougainvillea.

Above the Southern Nun Buoy,
hibiscus stars explode, dying angels,
while the *Isaac Allerton* rocks her keel

five fathoms and years beyond
green ripples of the cay.
I can see her tacking west
through the Straits of Florida,
Saint Elmo's fire cracking from her spars
before she broke on the reef.

My Love, what will wreckers find diving into the hold,
her ribs blooming rosettes of calcium?
What will they find in a hundred years
 of us,
our garish nights
on this spit of coral and palm.

FOLLOWING JESUS THROUGH THE EYE OF THE STORM

Somewhere around Sandusky, he blew by
in the fast lane—a white-streak, dually pickup,
car hauler in tow.
Something written big on the back of the box.
Being a sucker for even a bumper sticker,
you drop down to fifth & catch him:
If a man doesn't know Jesus
what can he say he really knows
I ask you, what kind of man would say a thing like that?

Bare arm dangling from the Hemi's cab window,
a barbecue cooker bound with bungee cords
under a flapping green tarp. Then the box trailer
about big enough for a redneck pole dancer's wedding.
You follow for miles wondering under
gathering doubt toward the Pennsylvania line.

The afternoon darkening since Michigan,
then rain drops across the Cuyahoga,
then rain and lightning, headlights & wipers, summer thunder
then darker, harder still.
Cars pulled over—flashers in the splash of Sunday—
wipers a full-tilt riot now. Back off
from water flooding the interstate's underpass.
He slows to seventy-five then holds it steady;
the man was damn good.

You had to give him that. The man was good or crazy
as hell or following Jesus as a Black & blind DJ
hollerin' psalms and secret commands over AM radio static.
Then you figure, "What the hell…"
crank it up, pull in and catch his slipstream tow.
Close enough, almost, to read the psalm in a swirl of storm-grey contrail.
Two ghosted forms across Ohio's landscape. Sweet baby Jesus,
did you have a drive till the storm blew over
that spindrift Sunday afternoon.

RED SOLO CUP

The pickup truck came along the dirt road near Abers Run, dust rising behind. When the road turned to gravel, the stones ricocheted off the undercarriage. At the rail crossing, the pickup stopped, and the driver's ponytail danced as she looked down the tracks. When she checked right she saw the old man on the seat beside her frowning. She let the clutch out before revving the engine and the truck lurched forward, stalled, then rolled backwards off the rise to the crossing.

Grandaddy, what should I do?

You the last one to touch the steering wheel, Sweet Pea. He coughed, then looked straight ahead.

She bit her lip. Set the e-brake, turned the key, picked up the revs and feathered the clutch. They banged and bounced forward across the tracks. She cautiously turned left on to West Virginia 37. She up-shifted slowly.

You mad at me, Granddaddy?

The old man had a hard look, not mean, but like he had seen a lot of the tough side of life. The green oxygen bottle and the plastic tubes over his ears going into his nose did little to allay that tempered look.

He pointed to the Dollar General lot. There, pull in!

Don't pussyfoot when you turn onto 37 like that. We don't need a logging truck making a hood ornament out of us. And I don't want to see you hitting the brakes two or three times like you want to do on bends and hills. Someday this state is going to be the biggest state in the union when politicians flatten it out, but until that time, I ain't gonna replace the front brakes more than I have to on this old girl.

They pulled back onto the highway.

Principal give you any trouble?

Principal Aldebrand, that old witch! She just said, Wanda, do you have to be all day?

I told her, doctor said my granddaddy got black lung and what's more can't drive no more. I got my permit so I can take him to the clinic in Wayne. Then she says, you're responsible to make up all the work you miss.

Yes'm, I said, and walked out of her office into the hallway stickin' my tongue out about as far as it could go.

Aldebrand, right? I worked with Randy and Keith down in a Mingo County mine till it closed down. Them three Aldebrand girls got to go to college and be teachers and such. The boys was just like me, wanted to work and buy a pickup with a tow hitch for a bass boat in the back. When we weren't fishing or working the mines, we'd be huntin'.

Granddaddy, you're the best teacher I could ever have. I'm the first one in my grade to get a driver's permit besides that big, old, dumb boy on the football team, and he has his license.

Do tell. Can't be that dumb if he passed his test before you.

Your mom hear from your pap lately?

Momma got some money about six months ago when he was at Detroit Diesel. You think he's comin' back? I miss Daddy so much.

If I was God, I could give you a better answer. You just keep helping your mother with your brothers and hope for the best. But keep helping. Lot of people take the *Hillbilly Highway* up to Detroit then come back.

Why were you frowning at me back at the railroad crossing?

Wasn't you. Those rusty tracks got me thinking. Don't give a damn what old man Trump says. Coal ain't coming back. They hauled the long-wall mining machine out of Cordelia # 2 last year, probably shipped to China. Coal ain't king no more. Even them tracks running through the middle of Wayne are rusty.

Granddaddy, you like that Toby Keith song?

Sure do, Sweet Pea. What's it called again? How 'bout you sing a few bars?

It goes, *Red Solo cup, I fill you up. Let's have a parrrr…* Shoot, I can't sing.

Yep, Patsy Cline wouldn' allow for such screechin'.

Oooh, you see that deer over there? Someone said you can eat them if you gut them in about two hours just like in the woods.

That's correct, but who in Hell would want to!

Granddaddy, they play Toby's song when you're on your exercise bike at the clinic!

When I'm huffin' and puffin' and that bike is squeakin' and I got that oxygen mask on my face lookin' like a handsome hog wearin' an ugly politician's false-face, I can't hear a damn thing.

Grandpa, you look beautiful to me! When I get out of high school, I am going to open an aerobics studio and you are gonna be my first and handsomest student and I am gonna play "Red Solo Cup" with Toby's other hits for my clientele all day long.

Little girl, with your flat fanny you'll look silly in them lizard-skin yoga pants, and if you want me, you may have to climb the hill to the cemetery above Cove Gap to get me.

She could feel the old man's hand touching her shoulder, but was so intent on watching the road in front of them like he taught her…

There's two generations of miners up there now. Your great-grandfather loaded more coal in a day than any man in Cordelia #1.

They say there's coal in a miner's veins, but hear me, Wanda, it's in my lungs hardin' like cement, the doctor says.

Grandaddy, I love when you talk to me like you talk to your buddies over coffee at the Wayne Diner.

The old man said, You watchin' your mirrors?

Then she glanced up. The west coast mirrors he hung on the pickup from an old junk log truck were filled with chrome, and flashing headlights.

Sweet Pea, pick it up! You gotta give him his head through these switchbacks and down the hill. Ain't no place to pull over and he's tryin' to make time to some damn where.

Granddaddy, I'm scared!

Git scared later. There's a big lot around the bend at the bottom and past the bridge. Put your signal on and hustle us down there.

She did what the old man said but now the semi's air horns seemed to be blasting in her ear. She bit down on her lip weaving through the bends down the hill.

Turn in fast, smooth. Don't jerk the wheel no matter what. That'll flip us.

The pickup charged into the gravel lot. The left front tire hit a depression, almost ripping the steering wheel out of her hands. The truck started to spin. She jammed the brake and clutch to the floor. The spin slowed as the circle tightened. Another rotation and they found themselves perched on the embankment over the creek at the far end of the Dew Drop Inn. But they stopped.

Her heart was pounding, her throat dry, stomach muscles tight. Slowly as her breath come back, she became aware of a hawk gliding across the field beyond the creek, autumn sunlight on its wings. Later she would remember the sound of her grandfather gulping air mixed with dust kicked up by their spin, his breathing tubes part way out of his nose, the green oxygen bottle ricocheting off the footwell. But the semi's air horns and squeal of tires, the flashing lights, were gone, at least for now.

She didn't look at him when the old man rasped, You, you want me to spell you at the wheel? I can drive okay with this oxygen.

She didn't answer for a minute, but then with a low, I'll git us there, Granddaddy.

At the edge of the highway, she looked left to where they had come too fast a few minutes ago—the concrete abutments. A dark presence still in the air, heavy, like the smell of sintered brake lining. The staccato of the truck's jake brake was their death rattle. But they had been spared today as if huge, black wings had passed over them. *Give us this day, our daily bread...*

That sumabitch, Grandpa said, he's probably late for lunch, that's all. An' you did a fair to middlin' good job on keepin' off that brake pedal.

She nodded, ran her tongue over the welt inside her mouth, the taste of blood. Then Wanda nailed the throttle. The Ford's back end twisted itself straight to her counter-steer, gravel spraying across 37 like birdshot. She grabbed second gear and pointed the truck right on toward Wayne.

NOTES

page 10   "Two-Lane Blacktop"

Inspired by the painting *Sunrise III*, W. Koral Sally Panza Gallery, Sept 2013

page 12   "Blacked Out Chrome"

During World War II, chrome trim on military vehicles and some civilian vehicles was darkened to prevent detection by the enemy.

Page 26   "Gather Ye Rosebuds"

Donna Mae Mims, first woman to win a Sports Car Club of America National Championship, 1963. She died in 2012 and at her request was laid out in her pink Corvette, which sported a large air-brushed picture of Marilyn Monroe on the hood. A portion of her ashes was scattered over the Cumberland, Maryland airport, site of the original Cumberland National Road Race where she participated in the '50s and '60s.

page 52   "Shanksville, Flight 93"

Give not up thy heart to sadness/ But drive it from thee/ For there is no returning/ And thou shalt do them no good... Ecclesiasticus, 38:21

page 56   "Talking Smack to the Dead"

Madness: a section at the Mid-Ohio road course. A short but abrupt rise. As the leading car crests the top, it disappears. At speed and in pursuit, this is immensely disconcerting to you the first time it occurs.

Page 64   "Clark's Lotus Grabbing Air"

Jimmy Clark, three-time world champion Formula 1 driver, from Scotland.

Juan Manuel Fangio, five-time world champion Formula 1 driver, from Argentina. He won the Cuban Gran Prix in 1957 but in 1958 watched the race as a "guest" of Castro's revolutionaries. He later commented it may have been a stroke of luck since the event was crash-riddled and several spectators were killed along the wet, treacherous, oceanside Malecon section.

Oh Shit: an extremely fast section of a mountain road at the Dureya Hillclimb. Modern production cars can reach 120 to 140 plus miles per hour. What is essentially a rural road ends in an abrupt, 300-degree bend.

Page 66   "The Completely Unheralded Jumping Frog of Calaveras County"

A riff on Twain's famous frog. Thanks, Samuel.

ACKNOWLEDGMENTS

The following works first appeared in the publications listed.

"Blacked-Out Chrome, 1945": *Rebuilding the Porch* (chapbook)

"Breakfast": *Rebuilding the Porch* (chapbook)

"Clark's Lotus Grabbing Air": *Edgz*

"The Chicken, The Road, The Woman": Westmoreland Heritage & Arts Festival, Podium Finish

"Click": *Moss Motoring*

"The Completely Unheralded Jumping Frog of Calaveras County": *Flashers Dozen*

"Grenade": *Eye Contact*

"Hand Dancing": *Pittsburgh Post-Gazette*

"In The Waiting Room of the Speedy Muffler King": *Pittsburgh Post-Gazette*

"Memorial Day, Ohio": *Fine Lines Journal*

"Plastic Jesus": *Loyalhanna Review*

"Shanksville, Flight 93": Westmoreland Arts & Heritage Festival, First Place

"Swing Low": *Pittsburgh Post-Gazette*

"Parkway Jam": *Pittsburgh Post-Gazette*

"Two-Lane Blacktop": *Uppagus*

"What He Remembers": *Depth-of-Field* (chapbook)

"The Women of Brick Alley": *Main Street Rag*

"Wreckage": *Depth-of-Field* (chapbook)

"Red Solo Cup": *Pine Mountain Sand & Gravel—Contemporary Appalachian Writing*

BIO

Walt Peterson has won the Acorn-Rukeyser award for poetry for *In the Waiting Room of the Speedy Muffler King* and the Gribble Publishing award for the collection of short fiction, *Depth-of-Field*. He has worked on projects such as the artist's book *Image/Song* and the show and anthology, *Fission of Form*, which was a collaboration of twenty sculptors, twenty illustrators and twenty poets. Peterson is a Fellow of the Western Pennsylvania Writing Project and a rostered artist with the Pennsylvania Council on the Arts. Lately, Peterson has published several creative nonfiction pieces including one, "Driving Pittsburgh," about racing in the Pittsburgh Vintage Grand Prix. He set the hillclimb record for Vintage 2 cars on Polish Mountain in his 1962 Austin-Healey 3000 and has been a performance driving instructor.

When my dad died, I was nineteen and I inherited a cool aunt, a set of Craftsman tools and a 1950 Buick. The Buick looked like a walrus with a full set of chrome teeth and a hood that was hinged on the side like a coffin. I learned to replace the blown three-speed transmission and patch and paint the rusty floor on the Green Monster, as my friends dubbed the car. It hauled us over Pittsburgh's wintry hills and took my aunt to family gatherings. Sadly, the Buick fell prey to bad brakes, no second gear (again) and the gleam in a junkman's eyes. The Craftsman hand tools are out in the garage workshop. Perhaps the Buick made it to an earthly car paradise like Havana, Cuba and exists still, independent of memory.

www.ingramcontent.com/pod-product-compliance
Lightning Source LLC
LaVergne TN
LVHW091616170726
843492LV00007B/2440